England

by Grace Hansen

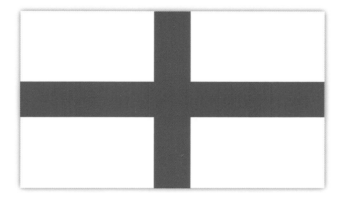

Abdo Kids Jumbo is an Imprint of Abdo Kids
abdobooks.com

abdobooks.com

Published by Abdo Kids, a division of ABDO, P.O. Box 398166, Minneapolis, Minnesota 55439.
Copyright © 2020 by Abdo Consulting Group, Inc. International copyrights reserved in all countries.
No part of this book may be reproduced in any form without written permission from the publisher.
Abdo Kids Jumbo™ is a trademark and logo of Abdo Kids.

Printed in the United States of America, North Mankato, Minnesota.

052019

092019

 THIS BOOK CONTAINS
RECYCLED MATERIALS

Photo Credits: AP Images, Getty Images, iStock, North Wind Picture Archives, Shutterstock

Production Contributors: Teddy Borth, Jennie Forsberg, Grace Hansen
Design Contributors: Dorothy Toth, Pakou Moua

Library of Congress Control Number: 2018963336
Publisher's Cataloging-in-Publication Data

Names: Hansen, Grace, author.

Title: England / by Grace Hansen.

Description: Minneapolis, Minnesota : Abdo Kids, 2020 | Series: Countries |
    Includes online resources and index.

Identifiers: ISBN 9781532185519 (lib. bdg.) | ISBN 9781532186493 (ebook) |
    ISBN 9781532186981 (Read-to-me ebook)

Subjects: LCSH: England--Juvenile literature. | Great Britain--History--Juvenile
    literature. | Europe--Juvenile literature. | Geography--Juvenile literature.

Classification: DDC 942--dc23

Table of Contents

England's History

England is a country in the United Kingdom (UK). The UK also includes Scotland, Wales, and Northern Ireland.

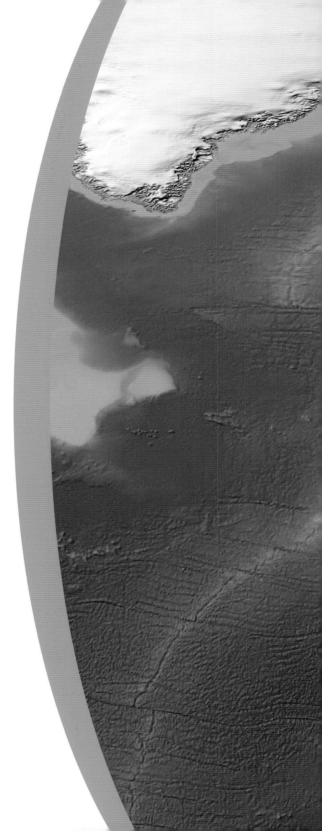

Northern Ireland

Scotland

Ireland

England

Wales

Europe

Atlantic
Ocean

Africa

5

Anglo-Saxons invaded England in the 5th and 6th centuries. They settled the land. The English language comes from many of their words.

7

England has a **constitutional monarchy**. **Parliament** makes laws. The king or queen is the head of state. The prime minister is the head of government.

Major Cities & Geography

The capital of England and the UK is London. London is also the largest city in the UK. More than 8.7 million people live there.

The River Thames flows through southern England, including London. The Tower Bridge stretches over it.

13

England is made up mostly of low hills and plains. Though the north and west is much hillier. The Pennine Hills are often called the "backbone of England."

Foods

England's **traditional** foods are simple. Popular foods include fish and chips and **Yorkshire pudding**. Many English people enjoy tea with milk and sugar.

Sports

Soccer is very popular in England. There, they call it football. Other popular sports include cricket and rugby.

19

Famous People

Two amazing authors were born in England. William Shakespeare wrote many plays, poems, and sonnets. J.K. Rowling wrote the Harry Potter series.

20

William
Shakespeare

21

Awesome Landmarks in England

Big Ben
London, England

Durdle Door
Dorset, England

Stonehenge
Wiltshire, England

White Cliffs of Dover
Kent, England

Glossary

Anglo-Saxon – a person of Germanic descent who lived in England before the Norman Conquest.

constitutional monarchy – a system of government in which a country is ruled by a king or queen whose power is limited by a constitution, or laws and rules.

Parliament – a group, made up of the House of Commons and House of Lords, that make laws for England.

traditional – relating to a culture's customs and ways of doing things.

Yorkshire pudding – a popover made of baked, unsweetened egg batter, typically eaten with roast beef.

Index

Abdo Kids
ONLINE
FREE! ONLINE MULTIMEDIA RESOURCES

Visit abdokids.com
to access crafts, games,
videos, and more!

Use Abdo Kids code

CEK5519

or scan this QR code!